What Do SCHOOL SECRETARIES Do?

Rita Kidde

PowerKiDS press.

New York

D0905552

Published in 2015 by The Rosen Publishing Group, Inc.
29 East 21st Street, New York, NY 10010

First Edition

Editor: Amelie von Zumbusch
Book Design: Colleen Bialecki
Photo Research: Katie Stryker

Photo Credits: Cover xPACIFICA/National Geographic/Getty Images; pp. 5, 9 Siri Stafford/Digital Vision/Thinkstock; p. 6 Christopher Robbins/Photodisc/Thinkstock; p. 10 Jack Hollingsworth/Stockbyte/Getty Images; p. 13 AtnoYdur/iStock/Thinkstock; p. 14 Yobro10/iStock/Thinkstock; p. 17 Nicholas Monu/E+/Getty Images; p. 18 JupiterImages/Polka Dot/Thinkstock; p. 21 Tina Stallard/The Image Bank/Getty Images; p. 22 Comstock Images/Stockbyte/Getty Images.

Publisher's Cataloging Data

Kidde, Rita.
What do school secretaries do? / by Rita Kidde. — 1st ed. — New York : PowerKids Press, c2015
        p. cm. — (Jobs in my school)
Includes an index.
ISBN: 978-1-4777-6935-5 (Library Binding)
ISBN: 978-1-4777-6538-8 (Paperback)
ISBN: 978-1-4777-6539-5 (6-pack)
1. School secretaries—Juvenile literature. 2. School secretaries.   I. Title.
LB2844.4.K57 2015
371.2

Manufactured in the United States of America

CPSIA Compliance Information: Batch # WS14PK4: For Further Information contact Rosen Publishing, New York, New York at 1-800-237-9932

CONTENTS

Do you know the **secretaries** at your school? They work in the office.

They need to be neat. They keep track of many things.

In some schools, they collect the lunch money. They may collect milk money, too.

They greet people who visit the school. **Visitors** may have to sign in.

They send out memos. These tell you about school events in the future.

They keep track of **student** files. Each file lists facts about a student.

Secretaries Day is in April. It is a day to honor their hard work.

If you are home sick, your mom or dad may need to call the secretary.

New students must talk to the secretary to sign up for school.

If you need to know
anything about the school,
ask them. They know a lot!

WORDS TO KNOW

secretary

students

visitor

WEBSITES

Due to the changing nature of Internet links, PowerKids Press has developed an online list of websites related to the subject of this book. This site is updated regularly. Please use this link to access the list: www.powerkidslinks.com/josc/secr/

INDEX